THE
2O13
GRIFFIN
POETRY
PRIZE
ANTHOLOGY

D0770505

PAST WINNERS OF
THE GRIFFIN POETRY PRIZE

2001
Anne Carson
Heather McHugh and Nikolai
Popov

2002
Christian Bök
Alice Notley

2003
Margaret Avison
Paul Muldoon

2004
August Kleinzahler
Anne Simpson

2005
Roo Borson
Charles Simic

2006
Kamau Brathwaite
Sylvia Legris

2007
Don McKay
Charles Wright

2008
John Ashbery
Robin Blaser

2009
A. F. Moritz
C. D. Wright

2010
Eiléan Ní Chuillieanáin
Karen Solie

2011
Dionne Brand
Gjertrud Schnackenberg

2012
Ken Babstock
David Harsent

The 2013 Griffin Poetry Prize Anthology

A SELECTION OF THE SHORTLIST

Edited by SUZANNE BUFFAM

ANANSI

Copyright © 2013 House of Anansi Press Inc.
Poems copyright © individual poets
Preface copyright © Suzanne Buffam

All rights reserved. No part of this publication may be reproduced or transmitted in any form
or by any means, electronic or mechanical, including photocopying, recording, or any
information storage and retrieval system, without permission in writing from the publisher.

This edition published in 2013 by
House of Anansi Press Inc.
110 Spadina Avenue, Suite 801
Toronto, ON, M5V 2K4
Tel. 416-363-4343
Fax 416-363-1017
www.houseofanansi.com

Distributed in Canada by
HarperCollins Canada Ltd.
1995 Markham Road
Scarborough, ON, M1B 5M8
Toll free tel. 1-800-387-0117

Distributed in the United States by
Publishers Group West
1700 Fourth Street
Berkeley, CA 94710
Toll free tel. 1-800-788-3123

House of Anansi Press is committed to protecting our natural environment.
As part of our efforts, the interior of this book is printed on paper made from
second-growth forests and is acid free.

17 16 15 14 13   1 2 3 4 5

Library and Archives Canada Cataloguing in Publication

Cataloguing data available from Library and Archives Canada

Library of Congress Control Number: 2013937210

Cover design: Brian Morgan
Cover image: Apollo Tended by the Nymphs, detail showing the head of Apollo, intended for
the Grotto of Thetis by Girardon, Francois (1628–1715) Chateau de Versailles, France/Peter
Willi/The Bridgeman Art Library
Typesetting: Marijke Friesen

Canada Council Conseil des Arts
for the Arts du Canada

ONTARIO ARTS COUNCIL
CONSEIL DES ARTS DE L'ONTARIO

We acknowledge for their financial support of our publishing program
the Canada Council for the Arts, the Ontario Arts Council, and the Government of Canada
through the Canada Book Fund.

Printed and bound in Canada

"A beauty not explicable is dearer than a beauty which
we can see the end of."
—Ralph Waldo Emerson, "The Poet"

CONTENTS

PREFACE

Imagine trying to pick your seven favourite birds on planet earth. How would you choose? Record their wingspans? Compare their calls in early spring? What set of fine-tuned, dispassionate criteria might you devise for this quixotic task? I, for one, have always been enchanted by the kingfisher, and while I could, if pressed, come up with a list of reasons why — its quizzical affect, for one thing, and the comic incongruity of its size and sense of sovereignty, for another — I am quite certain that any post hoc explanations would fail, in the end, to adequately account for my delight.

A book, of course, is no bird, no matter how many poets through the ages have invoked this quaint analogy. A work of art represents a complex set of choices made, more or less consciously, by an artist in response to a lengthy human history of such choices. It appeals not only to our senses but to our abstracting intelligence as well, and can be argued with on aesthetic, philosophical, and even moral grounds. Furthermore, it cannot fly, build a nest, or swallow a writhing amphibian in one gulp. And yet the question of enchantment remains.

"I have read almost all of Croce," wrote Borges of the Italian philosopher Benedetto Croce, whose thinking deeply influenced the aging Argentinian poet's early work, "and though I am not always in agreement with him, I am enchanted by him. Enchantment, as Stevenson said, is one of the special qualities a writer must have. Without enchantment, the rest is useless."

There comes a point, in other words, where all our objective criteria give way to something else — call it wonder, mystery, enchantment, awe — and it is at this numinous point of encounter that our dearest attachments are formed. The impossibility — or at least the wild improbability — of three separate individuals ever reaching true consensus on this point is no doubt exquisitely clear from the outset to the judges of any prize such as this one. And yet, far from obstructing the fulfillment of our task, this very diversity of attachments itself is what made the process of arriving at these shortlists so rewarding.

I am happy to report that I enjoyed an exchange of enchantments this winter with my fellow judges, Mark Doty and Wang Ping, whose considered selections and gentle, articulate queries caused me to grapple with my own inclinations and to reconsider books I'd overlooked. It is a telling detail about the ethos of this prize that nowhere on its website can you find a list of winners. Only the lists of books named to the annual shortlists appear. As many have already observed, after all, to be named to a shortlist for the Griffin Prize is, in many respects, already to have won. I am grateful to Mark and Ping for expanding my scope as a reader. I hope that readers of this anthology will discover in its pages new enchantments of their own.

Meanwhile, to those who shake their heads and lament the decline of poetry, I offer this parting observation: while the number of species of birds on this planet — which now hovers somewhere just over ten thousand — may be in irrefutable decline, the number of books submitted every year to the Griffin Prize for Excellence in Poetry — fast approaching six hundred in this, its thirteenth, year — continues to rise.

Suzanne Buffam, March 2013

INTERNATIONAL
FINALISTS

FADY JOUDAH *(translator)*

GHASSAN ZAQTAN

Like a Straw Bird It Follows Me, and Other Poems

What does poetry do? Nothing and everything, like air, water, soil, like birds, fish, trees, like love, spirit, our daily words… It lives with us, in and outside us, everywhere, all the time, and yet, we are too often oblivious of this gift. It's a poet's job to bring this gift out and back, this gift that makes us human again. And Mr. Zaqtan has done it. His poetry awakens the spirits buried deep in the garden, in our hearts, in the past, present, and future. His singing reminds us why we live and how, in the midst of war, despair, global changes. His words turn dark into light, hatred into love, death into life. His magic leads us to the clearing where hope becomes possible, where healing begins across individuals, countries, races…and we are one with air, water, soil, birds, fish, trees…our daily words pregnant with beauty, and we begin to sing again till "…the singer / and the song / are alike" ("Biography in Charcoal"). This is Mr. Zaqtan's only "profession." It's now also ours. About the translation: as a translator of poetry myself, I know the danger, frustration, and the joy in the process of catching the fire from the original and delivering it through/into another language, another culture, another sentiment. Mr. Joudah delivered with such grace and power. My salute to Mr. Joudah, as translator to translator, as poet to poet, as doctor to doctor. — Wang Ping

The Dead in the Garden

Don't open the window
don't wake up
I beg you don't wake up…
they were dancing on the garden grass
as if they were the garden's motive
or its meditation
and they were screaming there

Beneath the light
their dust was coming apart

it had rained at night
all night.

Black Horses

The enemy's dead think mercilessly of me in their eternal sleep
while ghosts take to the stairs and house corners
the ghosts that I picked off the road and gathered like necklaces
from others' necks and sins.

Sin goes to the neck...there I raise my ghosts, feed them
and they swim like black horses in my sleep.

With the energy of a dead person the last blues song rises
while I think of jealousy
the door is a slit open and breath enters through the cracks, the river's
respiration, the drunks
and the woman who wakes to her past in the public garden

     and when I fall asleep
   I find a horse grazing grass
      whenever I fall asleep
   a horse comes to graze my dreams.

On my desk in Ramallah there are unfinished letters and photos of
    old friends,
a poetry manuscript of a young man from Gaza, a sand hourglass,
and poem beginnings that flap like wings in my head.

I want to memorize you like that song in elementary school
the one I carry whole without errors
with my lisp and tilted head and dissonance...
the little feet that stomp the concrete ground with fervor
the open hands that bang on desks

All died in war, my friends and classmates...
and their little feet, their excited hands, remained
stomping the classroom floors, the dining tables and sidewalks,
the backs and shoulders of pedestrians...
wherever I go
I hear them
I see them.

An Enemy Comes Down the Hill

When he comes down
or is seen coming down
when he reveals to us that he is coming down.

The waiting and silence

his entire lack
when he hearkens before the plants.

His caution when he comes down
like one postponed by a hush,
and by his being not "us"
and not "here"
death begins.

He bought a flower
nothing more, a flower
that has no vase and leaves no will.

From the hill, he can spot the military checkpoint, the paratroopers,
he can spot the squatters, the mountain edges, and the only road
where their feet will leave a print in the rocks, mud, and water.

Losses also will appear from the hill
abandoned without effort.

And the fragility in shadow,
the Jewish man with a long mustache
who resembles the dead Arabs here.

From the mountain edges, all the caves will appear peaceful
and the road will seem as it were.

While he was coming down
the caves continued to stare
and blink in the cold.

The Orchard's Song

Dear daughter
when you go to pick the quince
don't wake me

I've been dead for a long time, as you know,
like an ancient summer I sleep on a cold stone,
the sun turns me to the right and to the left
and the birds peck my head

Light passed me to shadow
shadow to light

…and the languages and dialects of slaves
used to fill the night when I passed,
and their amulets held the memories
and dragged them as if a swarm of ants

The singers' tambourines were swimming like a raft
around the radiance
lifting me in a joyous air,
and I was by the orchard's edge, the quince orchard,
reading an ode, perhaps by the captive prince:

I wish you'd turn serene.

The Bird Follows Me

In the year two thousand or a little before, there might have been
a prelude that inhabited me, it resembled summer
in the rooms of bachelors,
I used to spin it in my speech

like a pleasant gait on an edge of marble, or dusting it
from what the hooves of mules leave behind
as they climb the wadi

"…in my house
women give birth to rings
and disappear from the world beyond the door,
here's the paradise of the one I love
and the journey
of the one who saw…"

A prelude like other preludes
I didn't retrieve from muttering

Like a straw bird
it follows me.

Everything As It Was

What led him over there
in such cold weather?
Not longing or curiosity
but maybe fear or perhaps it was
the chill in the room,
though everything appeared as it was,
as he wrote in an old poem he could not finish

"...Everything is still as it was
since we had gone out to war,
since childhood or before,
perhaps the sun of those years made the white curtains grow
fainter, and the pebbles
in the hallway became rounder
and shinier or the grass had grown longer
or dried up!

"The three mirrors are as they were
the sheets, the shelf
and the broom

"the family photo
the leather-bound Quran
the rosary of the deceased grandmother

"everything was as if nothing had changed.
Perhaps we
we who fell upon the war
from the school bell..."

That was in the summer of 1986 in Damascus, his mother was still
    alive then
and there was an opening somewhere in that poem, more like a
    hole that followed him,
he'd hear it stumble behind him wherever he went, especially
    when toward the anxious
endings in his dreams, and even there, they, the boys, would
    continue to stare at him
and send out their perplexing gestures, the boys who did not
    return after the midnight
patrols, and the dead who went back to sit on the doorsteps of
    their houses

Now he feels a saunter in him through that opening,
without knowing exactly where it is,
and where the poem is, in its painful incompleteness

Dampened with patience
overtaken by haste
he thought this kind of trickery
would befit the ending!

He could replace the "grandmother" with the "mother"
and observe
the disintegrating plaster above the door's awning
the upside down chair

where the mallow flowers stumble and recover
without being nursed
and the gentle light through the back window
remains in its same old place

Only the jasmine continued its climb, its eyes on the ceiling.

JENNIFER MAIDEN

Liquid Nitrogen

Jennifer Maiden's *Liquid Nitrogen* may very well be the most contemporary collection of poetry you'll ever read. Over the course of these dense, obsessive, and allegorical long poems, Maiden has created an absurdist theatre of global politics in which the spirits of public figures from across the last century share the stage with politicians, terrorists, dissidents, and fictional creations from our continuous present. Combining a free-wheeling, meditative style with crisp, lucidly elegant lines, Maiden's philosophical verse investigates the poetics of narrativity itself, not only as mediated by the news on TV, but by the no-less ethically charged realm of art as well. An extended meditation on the uses and abuses of power, the moral gravity of *Liquid Nitrogen* is buoyed throughout by Maiden's self-effacing sense of humor and her tenderness towards her grown daughter, Katharine, who stands at the heart of this collection. Epic in its scope and utterly eccentric in its approach, *Liquid Nitrogen* is a work of rare passion and unprecedented poetic achievement from one of Australia's most prominent living writers, "alert to the point of twitching," like the ox to whom she likens herself on page one, who nevertheless "still tramples through the difficult." — Suzanne Buffam

Hillary and Eleanor 9: The Pearl Roundabout

Eleanor Roosevelt woke up in Paris. Hillary
Clinton wore an autumn jacket, bright
beads, and addressed the Press about
the new Libyan No Fly Zone. Hillary's
campaign faux pearls — as big and
innocent as Jackie Kennedy's — were gone:
replaced by those semi-precious beads
in elegant earth colours, just
as Eleanor would have worn
herself. Hillary, however, did not
mention that this day in Bahrain
fifty demonstrators were shot, the Saudi
Army had moved in to savagely protect
the Government, with the glowing
Pearl Roundabout monument destroyed
because the protestors had employed
it as a gathering symbol. Eleanor
remembered the thirty-year-old statue
as being indeed quite as lovely
as a star turn at the jewellers,
the giant luna pearl enclasped
high up in petal-claws. Maybe
because she was old, she thought,
she increasingly loved the pretty.
            Hillary was actually
even prettier each day, but
the best she could attempt on Bahrain
was to recommend social order, the sacred
schoolday, workday. Eleanor had been
to school in France two centuries ago, the
headmistress a very nice American
Lesbian whose name she forgot, but

she did recall reading the Medieval
poem 'Pearl' on the pearl maiden lost
by her father as a child, reappearing as
an angelic young woman reproaching him
for not being a 'gentle jeweller', since
he mourned her inconsolably. We also,
Eleanor reflected, continue to grow
after death. Hillary at one point scratched
her head and visibly thought this would not
look so good and stopped. She often
scratched it absently, luxuriantly, as
women do, when she discussed her plans
with Eleanor. She could do anything in front
of her, she smiled with sugar, pretended it
was to the Press (some of whom suddenly
looked puzzled at her delicious fondness),
told all who were staying to enjoy
their night in Paris teasingly, then left.
Her cute march out of the room, smile
were as self-consciously naughty as a moppet
in the movies, so relaxed
because Eleanor was there. As soon
as they were in the hotel room, she knew
as useful as the Seine, she'd hear
'But, now, about Bahrain, my dear…'
and thankfully it would not let her be.

In the International Pavilion

In the International Pavilion,
for carven cats there are three positions
mainly: the sleeping round, the sphinx
and the sitting upright Bast,
protector of women. These cats
are painted in African sunset
colours, from bird pink to black,
with russets, grapes and tangerines.
They look edgy, like the live
exhibits. The Show is always
edgy, its moon often a high
cold full Easter moon. Some of the
animals will die and be tasted
and fear it. Some schoolchildren
who bred them will vomit with pride.
            Katharine and I avoid
the live exhibits these days, even
the pretty petting zoo. We buy a small pride
of soapstone for her cat collection, two
hippos for my soapstone hippos,
too. These hippos are different:
curled asleep like cats, not upright
on four legs with flaring noses.
When Katharine was a baby, I wrote
a poem that cats have small dry
noses and dogs large wet ones. Mysteriously,
it was requested for an erotic
international anthology and I agreed
diplomatically. Katharine still
finds that hilarious, but I suppose
the anthologists could have been northern
from some area of ice where noses

chill easily and need a pridelike welcome.
I try to photograph her with the new
digital camera but it has too
funhouse a dimension, distorts
the nose too far before the face, which
should suit the Show, but I abandon
it for the mobile phone, which shows
that moon of equinox behind her better, and
her small fine straight nose with its
slight nostril flare in proportion.
We buy a round white cloth cat:
mouthless, Japanese and strong,
the lack of mouth suggesting not
docility but a placid and wide
powerful telepathy. It has
a nose, which looks sensitive and neat.
Such cats were strewn around
the Japanese tidal wave wreckage, wet
and no doubt radioactive. Urbane men
with grim in their name and tone spoke
on Western TV saying that
the Japanese crisis would prove
the safety of nuclear power. Stray
toy cats without mouths did not
lower their pride to reply. The grim moon
of April is a pale pear blossom, not
pink like cherry, peach or plum. Somewhere
here a cow lows, uncertain. We
hope it is a dairy cow, move on
in the milk-warm moon of caution.

Diary Poem: Uses of Liquid Nitrogen

Somewhere in this poem, I may be going to tell
you that Grace Perry boasted that
her sperm was better than Malcolm Fraser's,
which claim she indeed made, but its
context is milder. Grace had dumped editing
Poetry Australia on Les Murray and grown rapt
at breeding better cattle by artificial
insemination in the Berrima Valley, most
of which she owned. She saw Fraser's
cattle breeding as the one to beat and wanted
to top his reputation as she brought
truckloads of sperm in milky daylight
to courteous cows. These days, human sperm
is frozen in liquid nitrogen, better
than ordinary ice, but I'm not sure Grace
froze her bull sperm and, if so, in what.
Somewhere in this poem, I may describe
a beautiful experiment in magnetism
and quantum physics in which a disc
magnet covered in shining ice has
been frozen in liquid nitrogen and hovers
in free air above a magnetised plank
and behaves as the owner wishes, positions
itself at desired angles, floats and floats.
                    Lyricism
is about positioning. I remember
Brenda Beaver expressing her love
for the music of Tear and Ferrier because
they 'stole up' on the high notes. When Bruce
and Bren babysat Katharine they all happily
watched *Brigadoon* since Bruce declared
'All little girls love ballet,' Lyricism

takes a little time and planning. Else
where, I have written how the computers
at Langley are so large they have to be kept
in liquid nitrogen not to overheat, that it's in
                    there
they are trying to trap Assange. Thinking of Grace,
somewhere here I may try my hand at literary
reminiscences, remember how she said James
Dickey had destroyed his pancreas with grog
and therefore wrote *Deliverance*, but I'm
not sure what she had against the book: maybe
just that he'd declined into prose. She had
him as a house guest, brought him a glass
of passionfruit juice one morning and he cried, 'My
God, woman, take it away. There are eyes
in it!' but that seems to me quite
a legitimate response to passionfruit and not
evidence of drunken paranoia. The doctor
in Grace could overcome the poet, if her verse
these days is underrated, with its note
of poems being spartan necessity, 'frozen
sections' that all medicine requires. She never
knew what to do with me, encouraging me but
disliked anything like a female rival, with
eyes in it, although I'm sure I just
floundered around as usual, an ox not
seeing myself as a threat — which, of course,
I wasn't, and am not. Somewhere in this poem,
I may insert George and Clare because
Assange told some gullible journo who wrote
his biography that his white hair
was the result of an accident with a cathode
ray tube in his teens. And no doubt Clare
to George's amusement could now be saying to all
that her white hair had the same cause, not

its real source in trauma. Liquid nitrogen
— the use of the frozen suspension which is risky
but also fecund and has beauty — is how
I would see those of my poems in which public
figures discuss things with their inspirations,
not for example that I've 'shredded' Gillard's
'interest in Nye Bevan', as some critic
perhaps strategically misunderstood. Liquid
nitrogen does not shred, it facilitates,
should not be exclusive to Satan, to Langley, is
too good. Yeats feared falling
from oneself, not seeing the Prince of Chang
in one's dreams anymore. Liquid nitrogen
as in the poem provides the frozen dream
in which the two can talk again, inspirer
and inspired. Nor do you reading over-accelerate
the pace of what I have to say, so
somewhere in this poem I could
tell you again that the language binary
of computers is the same as that of poems:
that the second process is the first, raw magic
of electrons responding to language, memorising
verse, its algorithms as careful,
logo-rhythms, not
even a metaphor, but just the inner
blood beat in the synapse, memory's clay,
and somewhere in this poem, I may.

My heart has an Embassy

My heart has an Embassy
for Ecuador where I will seek
asylum. Earthquakes
and aftershocks undermine
my hope and my means to work
and the Americans
have wormed into my psyche
with their black knack at fear.
My heart has an Embassy
for Ecuador as rare in air
and sumptuous as the Andes,
as clear as the Equator. There
will be in it waterfalls
and jungles like salvation.
There will be friends
whom I owe nothing, no
famed bail, no knotty
knowing sexualities. My heart
has an Embassy for Ecuador
where there will be no secrets
and the truth falls down like water
from giant granites of despair.

ALAN SHAPIRO

Night of the Republic

This extraordinary poetic sequence, Alan Shapiro's eleventh book, is an attempt to enter and diagnose a pervasive emptiness at the heart of contemporary American life. Shapiro's unwavering gaze fixes on vacant public spaces at night — parking garage, car lot, park bench, gas station men's room — and finds in those absences a way to read the marks of human presence, the scuffs and scars and damages that reveal the vulnerability that lies beneath our ambition, our hurry, and our disregard. These meditative, syntactically supple lyrics bring a new level of abstraction and of sophistication to this poet's work, marking a maturation of an already accomplished style that makes him a poet commensurate with the strange, aching, exhilarating spaces of modernity. — Mark Doty

Gas Station Restroom

The present tense
is the body's past tense
here; hence
the ghost sludge of hands
on the now gray strip
of towel hanging limp
from the jammed dispenser;
hence the mirror
squinting through grime
at grime, and the worn-
to-a-sliver of soiled soap
on the soiled sink.
The streaked bowl,
the sticky toilet seat, air
claustral with stink —
all residues and traces
of the ancestral
spirit of body free
of spirit — hence,
behind the station,
at the back end of the store,
hidden away
and dimly lit
this cramped and
solitary carnival
inversion — Paul
becoming Saul
becoming scents
anonymous
and animal; hence,
over the insides
of the lockless stall

the cave-like
scribblings and glyphs
declaring unto all
who come to it
in time: "heaven
is here at hand
and dark, and hell
is odorless; hell
is bright and clean."

Car Dealership at 3 A.M.

Over the lot a sodium aura
within which
above the new cars sprays
of denser many-colored brightnesses
are rising and falling in a time lapse
of a luminous and ghostly
garden forever flourishing
up out of its own decay.

The cars, meanwhile, modest as angels
or like angelic
hoplites, are arrayed
in rows, obedient to orders
they bear no trace of,
their bodies taintless, at attention,
serving the sheen they bear,
the glittering they are,
the sourceless dazzle
that the showcase window
that the showroom floor
weeps for
when it isn't there —

like patent leather, even the black wheels shine.

Here is the intense
amnesia of the just now
at last no longer longing
in a flowering of lights
beyond which
one by one, haphazardly
the dented, the rusted-through,

metallic Eves and Adams
hurry past, as if ashamed,
their dull beams averted,
low in the historical dark they disappear into.

Hotel Lobby

Light the pursuer, dark the pursued.
Light wants to fill dark with itself
and have it still be dark
so light can still be filling it.
Light pours from the massive shining of the chandelier
over the bronze boy bending beneath it
to the bronze pool where a watery face
is rising to meet his as he bends.
Light the pursuer, dark the pursued,
along the naked back and arms,
the hands, the fingers reaching
for the rippling features, just
beyond, just out of the grasp of
into and out of, and across
the marble floor and pillars,
to the tips of leaves, and up
the lion claws of chair legs and sofas and
over the glass tops of tables in the lounge,
light losing dark by catching it,
dark giving light the slip by being caught,
on elevator doors, down every
blazing hallway to the highest floor,
the farthest room, and through it
beyond the pulsing colors of the muted screen,
from hip to hip in a loose twilight
of sheets no longer shifting.

Stone Church

A space to rise in,
made from what falls,
from the very mass
it's cleared from,
cut, carved, chiseled,
fluted or curved
into a space
there is no end to
at night when
the stained glass
behind the altar
could be stone too,
obsidian, or basalt,
for all the light there is.

At night, high
over the tiny
galaxy of candles
guttering down
in dark chapels
all along the nave,
there's greater
gravity inside the
the grace that's risen
highest into rib
vaults and flying
buttresses, where
each stone is another
stone's resistance to
the heaven far
beneath it, that
with all its might

it yearns for, down
in the very soul
of earth where it's said
that stone is forever
falling into light
that burns as it rises,
cooling, into stone.

Funeral Home

After the last mourners,
and the dumping out
of flowers and the polishing
and vacuuming and
sweeping up before
it starts all over again tomorrow,
a white owl keeps watch
from within his tree
within the carpet
while dust motes — stirred up
like silt in water
by the constant going
in and out all day,
the sitting and the rising —
finally reach their peak
and turn to float
back down so slowly
that the empty vases
in the dark could be
the flowers themselves,
the blossoms that have
just now opened wide
for the dry rain
that will fill them
all around the owl
on the spotless breakfront
and between the chairs
and couches and on either
side of the doorways to the
family room, the chapel,
and the roped-off staircase
which if not for the rope

could be a staircase in an inn
made to look like a home
made to look like a mansion
where no one lives.

Beloved

The block is empty. I'm the boy there in the street,
Looking downhill for you to turn the corner,
Out of the avenue where horn blare, veils

Of exhaust, and strangers in a hurrying sleepwalk
Through each other tell me you'll be here soon.
And soon is home, and home is when at last

Your any moment now sensation brings
Out of the day's dull glint and inching flow
The look and bearing of a just for me

Unearned, unjustified, imagined face
That's all I need, so long as it's arriving,
That's mine till your real face effaces it.

But not today, not now, not ever again.
No one but me is left here outside the house
Where you by being dead are more alive

To me than ever, you who have no other
Purpose now, no other way of being,
Than to appear by never quite appearing,

Whenever I need you, any time I want
Clearer and still clearer in the aftermath
Of your not yet but soon about to happen.

Faucet

The faucet dripped one slow drip from its lip,
A slight convexity at first of metal
Distilled from metal to a silvery blur,

Opaque as mercury, that thickened to
A see-through curvature, a mound that swelled
As streams I couldn't see poured in and filled it,

Stretched by its own weight to a rounder shape
That grew less round the heavier it grew,
A tiny sack of water filled by water,

Held by water trembling as it clung
And dangled, swaying, till it snapped in two,
And one part plummeted and the other sprung

Back to the lip and grew all over again.
I told myself if I could just remember
The way the trembling surface tension full

Of surface tension hung there till it didn't,
Till it did again, somehow the house,
And everything and everyone within it,

The very moment of that day and year,
All of it, every bit would return to me
Exactly as it was. And I did. And it didn't.

BRENDA SHAUGHNESSY

Our Andromeda

Brenda Shaughnessy, in her third collection, continues to work the rich verbal surfaces and punning, allusive textures that marked her previous work, but her art has been transformed by a galvanizing sense of necessity into a more riveting, sometimes fiercely direct consideration of what it is to love a child, to care for one whose ability to care for himself is profoundly limited. What Wallace Stevens called "the pressure of reality" has deepened and furthered the work of a poet whose early poems indeed might have come from the same well as *Harmonium*. Without losing her music, playfulness, or sass, Shaughnessy has established herself as a poet of breathtaking emotional depth; to read such clear, affirming song made out of love, grief, and danger is both devastating and uplifting at once.
— Mark Doty

Artless

is my heart. A stranger
berry there never was,
tartless.

Gone sour in the sun,
in the sunroom or moonroof,
roofless.

No poetry. Plain. No
fresh, special recipe
to bless.

All I've ever made
with these hands
and life, less

substance, more rind.
Mostly rim and trim,
meatless

but making much smoke
in the old smokehouse,
no less.

Fatted from the day,
overripe and even
toxic at eve. Nonetheless,

in the end, if you must
know, if I must bend,
waistless,

to that excruciation.
No marvel, no harvest
left me speechless,

yet I find myself
somehow with heart,
aloneless.

With heart,
fighting fire with fire,
flightless.

That loud hub of us,
meat stub of us, beating us
senseless.

Spectacular in its way,
its way of not seeing,
congealing dayless

but in everydayness.
In that hopeful haunting
(a lesser

way of saying
in darkness) there is
silencelessness

for the pressing question.
Heart, what art you?
War, star, part? Or less:

playing a part, staying apart
from the one who loves,
loveless.

All Possible Pain

Feelings seem like made-up things,
though I know they're not.

I don't understand why they lead me
around, why I can't explain to the cop

how the pot got in my car,
how my relationship

with god resembled that
of a prisoner and firing squad

and how I felt after I was shot.
Because then, the way I felt

was feelingless. I had no further
problems with authority.

I was free from the sharp
tongue of the boot of life,

from its scuffed leather toe.
My heart broken like a green bottle

in a parking lot. My life a parking lot,
ninety-eight degrees in the shade

but there is no shade,
never even a sliver.

What if all possible
pain was only the grief of truth?

The throb lingering
only in the exit wounds,

though the entries were the ones
that couldn't close. As if either of those

was the most real of an assortment
of realities — existing, documented,

hanging like the sentenced
under one sky's roof.

But my feelings, well,
they had no such proof.

Liquid Flesh

In a light chocolatine room
with blackout windows,
a loud clock drowns in soft dawn's

syllables, crisscrossed
with a broken cloudiness
I'd choose as my own bedcovers

but cannot. My choice of sleep
or sky has no music of its own.
There's no "its own" while the baby cries.

Oh, the baby cries. He howls and claws
like a wrongly minor red wolf
who doesn't know his mother.

I know I am his mother, but I can't
quite click on the word's essential aspects,
can't denude the flora

or disrobe the kind of housecoat
"mother" always is. Something
cunty, something used.

Whatever meaning the word itself
is covering, like underwear,
that meaning is so mere and meager

this morning. Mother. Baby.
Chicken and egg. It's so obnoxious
of me: I was an egg

who had an egg
and now I'm chicken,
as usual scooping up

both possibilities,
or what I used to call
possibilities. I used

to be this way, so ontologically
greedy, wanting to be it all.
Serves me right.

My belief in the fluidity
of the self turns out to mean
my me is a flow of wellwater,

without the well, or the bucket,
a hole dug and seeping.
A kind of unwell, where

the ground reabsorbs
what it was displaced to give.
The drain gives meaning to the sieve.

As I said: a chicken who still
wants to be all potential.
Someone who springs

and falls, who cannot see
how many of us I have
in me — and I do not like them all.

Do I like us? Can I love us?
If anyone comes
first it's him, but how can that be?

I was here way, way first.
I have the breasts, godawful, and he
the lungs and we share the despair.

For we are a we, aren't we? We split
a self in such a way that there isn't
enough for either of us.

The father of the baby is sleepy
and present in his way, in the way
of fathers. He is devoted like

few fathers and maybe hurts
like I hurt, like no fathers.
I don't know what someone else

feels, not even these someones
who are also me. Do they hurt
like I do? Why can't they

tell me, or morse or sign: let
me know they know where and how
and why it hurts? Or something?

What is the point of other people,
being so separate, if we can't
help a person get that pain

will stick its shiv into anything,
just to get rid of the weapon
and because it can? For if we share

ourselves then they, too, must
also be in so much pain.
I can hear it. Oh, my loves.

The wood of the crib, the white
glow of the milk (which must
have siphoned off the one

and only pure part of me, leaving
me with what, toxicity
or sin or mush?), the awful softness.

I've been melted into something
too easy to spill. I make more
and more of myself in order

to make more and more of the baby.
He takes it, this making. And somehow
he's made more of me, too.

I'm a mother now.
I run to the bathroom, run
to the kitchen, run to the crib

and I'm not even running.
These places just scare up as needed,
the wires that move my hands

to the sink, to the baby,
to the breast are electrical.
I'm in shock.

One must be in shock to say so,
as if one's own state is assessable,
like a car accident or Minnesota taxes.

A total disaster, this sack of liquid
flesh which yowls and leaks
and I'm talking about me

not the baby. Me, this puddle
of a middle, this utilized vessel,
cracked hull, divine

design. It's how it works. It's how
we all got here. Deform
following the function…

But what about me? I whisper
secretly and to think,
around these parts used to be

the joyful place of sex,
what is now this intimate
terror and squalor.

My eyes burned out at three a.m. and again
at six and eleven. This is why the clock
is drowning, as I said earlier.

I'm trying to explain it.
I repeat myself, or haven't I already?
Tiny self, alone with a tiny self.

I'll say it: he hurt me, this new
babe, then and now.
Perhaps he always will,

though thoughts of the future
seem like science fiction novels
I never finished reading.

Their ends like red nerves
chopped off by cleaver, not aliens,
this very moment, saving nothing for later.

He howls with such fury and clarity
I must believe him.
No god has the power

to make me believe anything,
yet I happen to know
this baby knows a way out.

This dark hole closing in on me
all around: he'll show me
how to get through

the shock and the godlessness
and the rictus of crushed flesh,
into the rest of my life.

Hearth

Love comes from ferocious love
or a ferocious lack of love, child.

A *to* and a *from*, and an urgency,
a barefoot sprint in the high snow

for the only sagging shack in sight.
No doctor runs through the winter

woods at midnight to bring placebo.
But when he does it's just too late —

the house all fevered, grief the very
gifts of milk and stew and hearth

offered anyhow. How many tree
limbs are amputated by the self-

important sudden surgery of a gale —
those same limbs tortured further,

re-galed, as spirit-dancing fire?
But the trees don't experience it

the way it seems to me, like how
all that individual snow clumps

together because it is lonely
and trusts its kind. To be home

is to go somewhere, is velocity,
the same urgent comfort

of your name. You'll lack nothing,
child, and I will never let you go.

CANADIAN

FINALISTS

DAVID W. MCFADDEN

What's the Score?

"If the fool would persist in his folly, he would become wise," advised William Blake in his Proverbs of Hell. As if whispering through the ages into the ear of Canada's deadpan court jester, Blake's radical spirit slyly presides over David McFadden's exuberant thirty-fifth publication, *What's The Score?* With their arch yet affable tone, these ninety-nine irreverent and mock-earnest poems lay siege to the feelings of boredom, anxiety, and alienation that afflict a culture obsessed with wealth and prestige, leading us, again and again, down the road of excess to the palace of wisdom. "My poems go leaping from crag to crag," McFadden boasts in one poem, before quickly, and characteristically, scuttling this Romantic image of the egotistical sublime "like a stubble-faced crybaby, it's probably / because I've been writing for so long, / forty years of poems to various friends." The easy, casual intimacy of these poems will befriend you on the first page. Their astonishing leaps and their genuine philosophical urgency will compel you to keep reading. "Stick around," invites this artful and knowing wise fool, "everyone should have a chorus / following his steps and reminding him / of his central role in some great dream." — Suzanne Buffam

Stimulation Galore

Heavy winds and raining heavily though warm
this morning but this afternoon was sunny
and hot. Even the birds are singing with an
Italian accent. I'm in a tiny chapel
dedicated to a Madonna in 1580.

The mountains are dreams rising from the lake.
I lit a candle for luck in the church of St. Giacomo
where there's a thousand-year-old stone altar.
A marble life-size statue of Christ entombed.
The bull has a respectably long penis.

On the train a seventy-five-year-old man
wearing an excellent grey suit insisted
on having an elaborate conversation with me
in French all the way to Luxembourg.
He was a retired baker and a widower.

Poetry happens when language is used as a
device to broaden, deepen and intensify
the quality of emotion you are trying
to invoke in yourself. He showed me pictures
of his two children and five grandchildren.

He had no English but he recited beautifully
Rudyard Kipling's If in perfect French.
He got off at Brunelles and a tiny blond
grandma and her grandsons six and eight
got on and began giving me lessons in French.

They were going all the way to Como.
So when I got off I had lost all
my French and Italian and everything.
It's amazing how many people could not
muster up even one little word in English.

Not the station master or his personnel.
Not even the woman who sold tickets and cashed
my traveller's cheques. Not even bus drivers.
Not even the policeman who couldn't figure out
what to do with the fifty-year-old drunk.

The drunk was wearing a woman's dress and kept
pulling it up over his waist, exposing
nothing but his heavily stained trousers.
They didn't know what to charge him with
and everyone in the train began to shrug.

A beautiful woman came up to me and said,
"You are not a virgin and you have no child."
And then she said, "Let me be your child."
She lifted her dress and showed me a nasty bruise.
The bus to Bellagio had long ago gone.

I could hear the roaring waterfall
but couldn't see it no matter how I tried.
The men in the Bar Milano in Nesso
glanced at me but they didn't know
beans about the wonderful English language.

My complete and utter lack of Italian
was no laughing matter at the time.
In flashes Italian mountains made me feel
very peculiar. As if I had lived forever.
As if I knew infinitely more than I know.

Right under my window a boat goes by.
It's the *Ninfen* of Lake Como (the *Water Lily*).
It's full of school kids, teachers and parents.
They're all wearing sunglasses. They are
looking in different directions but not up here.

All you need to know about a salamander —
you don't need to know how fast it can run.
We can see how fast it can run. It's obvious
they run so fast when a human comes wandering
down the path because we are so scary.

The lizard will lie in the cool darkness
waiting for the distant sound of dissolving
humans. And then he will spring to life
in the sun, listen to the birds singing.
Most men only want to drink and hold forth.

There are about a hundred young people
in the launch sailing beneath my window.
They're looking out in the many directions.
Soon they'll be hiding behind the trees
but still not a one has noticed me.

Italians have an intimate relationship
with Lake Como, more than others have
with the Great Lakes. They love it and they
are like children around it all the time.
They're all over in all manner of boats.

Sailboats, powerboats, speedboats, hydroplanes,
tourist launches, magnificent yachts, canoes,
strangely shaped one-of-a-kind inventions,
new imports from Japan, and the people
in bathing suits are stretched out and sunning.

Or maybe slathering oil on each other.
They feel no need to make any pretense
that they are not enjoying themselves immensely.
They go around in circles or they reconnoitre
in the middle of the lake to exchange news.

Like their boats, they come in all shapes
and agedness, youth and amount of tan.
Are desires inspired by the gods or do
humans make a god of their desire?
Shall we swim in circles or straight lines?

By arming ourselves with a knowledge of temporalia
we must avoid succumbing to temptations.
This implies a conscious controlled descent
into the underworld in order to see
how little good exists in the world of the flesh.

We extricate ourselves from being trapped.
To learn about the nature of vice is a virtue.
This is the story of Orpheus and wisdom
and Eurydice and concupiscence or passion.
It's always fun to swim in circles and lines.

Or as truth is disguised in fiction
or as the truths of philosophy may be
disguised or veiled in poetry. This morning
about four I had an attack of aphasia.
In my dream nobody had any sympathy.

And today I had another look at what
is my favourite painting at the Serbelloni.
The conversion of Saint Paul. It was a Bembo.
And the same look on Paul's face was on
Saint Francis's face as he receives the stigmata.

Is it truly a Bonifacio Bembo?
I wonder if they realize that it is.
I think he never even signed his paintings.
David, you talk too much. Stop talking and listen.
Many men when they reach your age start drinking.

They drink too much and forget
to listen. All they want to do is drink.
Their writing suffers terribly and they die.
At Victoria Station I'll never forget
the golden filigree in your eyes.

"You're going to have to let go of him now."
Pure gold, the porter telling us to move
with a minute left from the window to the door.
But now a boy of fourteen puts out his nets.
He's dressed only in a pair of jeans.

He's in a silver splendid twelve-foot outboard.
He stands and moves the oars a bit then throws
out another length of net. He'll sell
his catch to the local *ristorantes*.
Or maybe to the people at the Villa.

Thank God I've forgotten my desire for perfection.
It was in my blood, then one day it left me.
This is the picture of the way I was.
Now it's the only way I am in poems.
Perfection — and then I don't give a damn.

Then there's a tale about a white elephant.
Every poet at times must wonder if he's
a victim of a plot. Baraballo
was an elderly priest from Gaeta
who thought his verses were products of genius.

Petrarch had been publicly crowned on the Capitol
and Baraballo thought he should be too.
Pope Leo X who loved a nasty joke
offered his beloved elephant, Hanno,
to Baraballo so he could have a ride.

He rode from the Vatican to the Capitol,
dressed in a scarlet toga fringed with gold.
And to the sound of ninety-seven trumpets.
Hanno was a present from King Manuel
of Portugal — but Hanno became frightened.

Hanno stood trumpeting before the bridge
of Saint Angelo and refused to move.
Was it the shouts and cheers that frightened him?
Maybe the stench of the rotten corpses
that hanged from the gibbets of the castle.

We're told that elephants are highly sensitive.
The daily average was fourteen executions.
Maybe Hanno understood more deeply
and refused to go through with his role.
As for Leo, he thought he was a poet.

Chaucer visited Florence to check it out
and was told the Presbytery was the oldest
building in the world and he believed it.
I saw three paintings of the Virgin
in Mennagio, each with a sword in her hand.

On the western shore of the northern arm
of Lake Como everywhere I went
I carried a candle and thought about the saints
and their sufferings and innocence.
My suffering is negligible, believe me.

Whatever I get is more than I deserve.
No big deal but I wish I knew where you were
and I could up and go there straightaway.
Knock on your door, tell you how moved I was
by all those little golden sparkling tears.

Red flowers to the Virgin of Montserrat.
Portrayed *con bambino*. Jesus a golden saw,
with sawtooth mountains above the lake.
Below me the Italians scream with pleasure
as they go by in their little boats.

From now on I think I'll believe in God.
So many people refuse to believe.
Maybe they do but then pretend they don't.
Believing in God, believing you and me,
God believing all of us constantly.

Being bathed in the light of consciousness.
Never judging us but always the urge
to become beautiful and perfect.
This thought is born out of despair
into something easier to cherish.

Funny Country

In a funny country with no name
the dead are embalmed in such a way
they keep as fresh as a fallen log.

The living carry them here and there
to picnics or to the cricket match
and they engage them in dialogue.

In this lovely little land success
is all that folks are left with when
they don't try hard enough to fail.

Success goes hand in hand with shame
but failure has a nobler sort of name.
Success is something to condemn.

For it makes a fool of them and it
chokes them in their dark and dirty sleep.
Failure's grand and it's hard and deep.

Workout at the Why

Why go on?
Why head on here?
Why proceed on there?
Why knock on any door whenever you want?
Why wiener on wherever there's a western vista?
Why feel good about yourself when there's nowhere to go?
Why fail to notice when there's no horse to wrestle to the ground?
Why scrutinize the sky when it's full of harmless but unnecessary
    safeguards?
Why not continue when the streets are full of people screaming?
Why inquire about insinuations when all we're interested in is
    eating bananas?
Why be terrified when there are so many levels to vaporize?
Why go home when you could stay — if you're interested?
Why take an interest in saying no to a free lifetime supply of
    anything?
Why swim in dirty water if you could be ridiculed for thinking
    twice?
Why think deep thoughts if you could be treated in Tofino for shock?
Why get raped and beaten by gangs of unemployed fishermen if
    you can't outscale the opposition?
Why be nasty if there are no more male bastions in your homeland?
Why fornicate with your aunt and uncle now that offshore
    shopping has been terminated?
Why play the piano if you experience vertigo in the
    superabundance department?
Why force yourself to regurgitate whatever you want?
Why fear people who are part of a captive market?
Why not supplement your diet with meddlesome instruction
    manuals?
Why do the majority of men who wear Eau Sauvage complain to
    smooth-talking bartenders when they keep losing money in the

jukebox?

Why worry about your failing memory when the great Buddha in the sky won't allow you to forget anything he wants you to remember?

Why should the jackpot be bigger just because there were no winners last time?

Why not sit down and tell me how you got to be so thoughtful?

Why collect postage stamps when you could take broken laundromats to the dump?

Why say you're jealous when you're really not?

Why do the nicest people always hang around the bounds of bad taste?

Why do people with severe melanomas take an interest in cheap labour?

Microscopic Surgery

Going to stay some time before hopping
on the train all the way to Como.
Disoriented in London. It's so warm,
humid, but human, overcast and muggy.
Joy's not well, she got sick in Egypt.

String quartet at St. Dunstan's in Fleet Street.
Violinist cut her finger in a kitchen
accident and hadn't played for a year.
Microscopic surgery. Cut nerve.
But now she thinks she's going to be fine.

After the wine and cheese reception (tacky!)
(but nice) took picture of an old statue
of Queen Elizabeth (the first) that had just
been discovered in somebody's basement
and installed over the sacristy door.

Walking all through Westminster buying slides.
Weatherman on BBC-1;
Today most wet spots will become
dry and most dry spots will become wet.
Of course he said this with a smiling face.

JAMES POLLOCK

Sailing to Babylon

The sentence, in James Pollock's remarkably assured debut volume, is a unit of music and of time, a carefully modulated choreography that moves the reader through an elegantly constructed set of meditations on place and history and the education of the self — a self we come to know, in part, through the poet's evocation of a rich company of tutelary spirits: Glenn Gould and Northrop Frye, Henry Hudson and C. P. Cavafy. Quietly confident, formally adept, assured in their music, these artful lyrics are not only an accomplishment in themselves but promise to register, as the poet says, "the breaking changes of a life to come." — Mark Doty

Northwest Passage

after Cavafy
The Franklin Expedition, 1845–48

When you set out to find your Northwest Passage
and cross to an empty region of the map

with a headlong desire to know what lies beyond,
sailing the thundering ice-fields on the ocean,

feeling her power move you from below;
when all summer the sun's hypnotic eye

won't blink, and the season slowly passes, an endless
dream in which you're forever diving into pools,

fame's image forever rising up to meet you;
when the fall comes, at last, triumphantly,

and you enter Victoria's narrow frozen Strait,
and your *Terror* and *Erebus* freeze in the crushing floes;

in that long winter night among the steeples
of jagged ice, and the infinite, empty plain of wind and snow,

when the sea refuses to be reborn in spring,
three winters pass without a thaw, and the men,

far from their wives and children, far from God,
are murdering one another over cards;

when blue gums, colic, paralysis of the wrists
come creeping indiscriminately among you;

and you leave the ships, and set out on the ice,
dragging the lifeboats behind, loaded

with mirrors and soap, slippers and clocks,
into the starlit body of the night,

with your terrible desire to know what lies beyond;
then, half-mad, snow-blind, even then,

before you kill the ones who've drawn the fatal lots,
and take your ghastly communion in the snow,

may you stumble at last upon some band of Inuit
hauling their catch of seal across the ice,

and see how foolish you have been:
forcing your way by will across a land

that can't be forced, but must be understood,
toward a passage just now breaking up within.

The Poet at Seven

If only he could watch his teacher read
and, gazing, could lean there at his desk
in the winter light of Hillcrest Public School
and listen as she speaks the strangest words —
with her vivid face, her braided hair
and dark eyes like a real and ordinary
siren's — if only he could wait like that
forever while Miss Harmon reads *The Odyssey*
(his kind young teacher with the ringing voice
he loves so much he lets the story sing
into his heart), she would peal out for him,
swaying above him like a slender bell,
the breaking changes of a life to come.

Ex Patria

Some nights I stand before my bookcase,
touching the spines. The household gods
are murmuring in their sleep.

At last I take a volume,
open its paper cover
like a hatch, and my mind climbs down

to the half-remembered
country I have left:

the same ethereal smell of cold,
the same snow-light in the air
from the blue snow squeaking underfoot,

the same flakes falling in the silent road
among branches of the silver maple
where the scarlet cardinal shakes himself and sings.

I want to take it all in,
and I do — so far in, so strangely
and imperfectly inside me

it has to change itself to be there
because I've changed.
A fresh breeze rises

in the branches. The cardinal utters
something through his mask. It's too much.
I close the hatch.

House

Its glassy look suggests one hypnotized
from gazing at the house across the street
as if into a mirror: a man half-crazed
with disappointed love. Look how distraught

after the vivid morning he appears
now in the gathering shade of afternoon,
how filled with darkness, how the darkness pours
like flames in silence out of every pane

across the unmowed lawn into the trees.
But when the stifling air grows vague with dusk,
and the sky is overwhelmed with cloudy towers
that blot the stars like battlements of dust,

the boy inside turns on the lights and sings
the sympathy of not inhuman things.

The Museum of Death

In the Museum of Death the guests are eating lunch
made from a dead man's recipe.
They use knives and forks invented by the dead.

Everyone sits in a room
built by those who are no longer with us,
everyone speaking words the dead have made.

Everything is archaeological:
prayer, toilets, table manners, cash.
Even the air was once breathed by the dead.

Look how impatiently the curator taps
his fingers on his desk. It's getting late.
Very soon the guests will have to go.

Northwest Passage

Henry Hudson, his final voyage, 1610–11

If you should fail to find your passage north
across the Arctic Ocean to Cathay,

and fail again to find your northeast passage
above the frozen coast of Muscovy

beyond Nova Zembla and the Gulf of Ob,
then fail heartbreakingly in seeking westward

two hundred miles upriver at Norumbega
until your good ship almost runs aground;

and if you should rig again your old *Discovery*,
trimming your sails for your northwest way at last,

and cross the sea to Resolution Island,
that most fog-laden threshold in the world,

and drive into the Furious Overfall
foaming in the mouth of that forbidding strait

drawn on the map by those who sailed before you
that far only, threading your delicate way

through a labyrinth of ice-floes in the wind,
a nightmare of rain and cloud, fog and snow,

and mutiny kindling and covered in the cabins;
and if, steering by heaven and your compass,

you should name the towering landmarks as you go —
Desire Provoketh and, some leagues beyond,

Cape Hopes Advance, the island Holde with Hope;
yea, if a huge wind plow the booming ice

against you, till you set anchor for safety
far to the south in a vast but dead-end bay

and freeze there all that winter in the dark;
in your desperation, before you make a plan

in secret to explore some other way
and set out in the shallop in the spring,

leading your own personal mutiny
against yourself by leaving your command;

before you come back having failed again;
before the last rebellion of your starving crew

drives you back to the shallop with your son,
your mate, and five mariners, sick and lame,

and sails guilty and terrified back to England;
haul anchor, sailor, trim your sails for home,

and, before you raise Cape Hopes Advance,
name the breaking ice-field Patience Bay.

Map of the Interior

The explorer David Thompson (1770–1857)

I like to think how he prepared himself
for fifty thousand miles of traveling

on foot and by canoe by reading books.
A Grey Coat Schoolboy off Westminster Abbey.

Gulliver's Travels, Robinson Crusoe,
the Persian and Arabian Nights. (He says

in his book somewhere that *Hudson Bay is
a place Sinbad the Sailor never saw,*

as he makes no mention of Musketoes.)
I see him peering through his microscope

at the two-piece *Musketoe Bill* (whose upper shaft
is black, three-sided, sharp; the lower *a round*

*white tube like clear glass; and the mouth inverted
upwards. For with the upper part the skin*

*is punctured, then the clear tube is inserted
in the wound.*) I picture him in the Rockies on

some vast defile of snow, his frightened men
boring a hole to see how deep the drift

lies under them. They can't plumb the bottom;
but he notices that perfect wound glows blue —

light near the surface, deepening to navy —
and wonders at the immensity of water

raised from the Pacific to that height,
salt ocean to fresh snow, *mysterious*

circulations on a scale so vast
the human mind is lost in contemplation.

In what year was he the first to comprehend
that huge system of interior plains

from which the Nelson and Saskatchewan
and Mackenzie, with all their tributaries,

pour their heart's blood out into the sea
like three titanic arteries of a body

supine as a sleeping giant's body?
All night he would lie beneath the stars

with a case of instruments, observing moon,
planets, constellations, breaking his quills

to calculate positions for the streams
and mountains, hills and lakes, and set them down

in numbers for translation to his map.
But a map's nothing but an image of the world

made small enough to hold inside the mind,
as different from the wilderness itself

as an anatomical chart is from a man.
His art was science — he never pretended

otherwise — even if the *voyageurs*
and Natives thought he could raise the wind

and saw the future through his telescope
and knew the men there and saw what they were doing.

For what he really knew he learned from them:
to give careful attention to all things,

the smallest stone, the bent or broken twig,
learned it from Native hunters in the field

for whom all such things spoke plain language.
For that was how you found your way at last

out of the great black forest to the place
exactly where you always meant to go.

IAN WILLIAMS

Personals

The moment I opened *Personals,* I was smitten. Mr. Williams is a musician. His words sing like brooks and streams through a virgin forest, laugh like waterfalls, startle and delight along the way with hidden eddies and boils. Mr. Williams is also an artist. His images fly like kites in the wind, with whistling somersaults. He blends personal emotion with historical tension, tradition and modernity, ordinary and magical so seamlessly. When he pulls the strings of contradictions: light and heavy, hilarious and serious, I can't help but dance like a happy puppet in the masterful hands. I'm so happy to find another shining star above Canada's poetry horizon! — Wang Ping

Rings

Problem is our armpits and crotches are feathered
with cobwebs. Problem is she leaks soft-boiled eggs
or I package seedless grapes. Problem is her parents
made us wait until they had crossed the width
of my nose. Problem is she had a migraine. Problem is
we did not want children. Problem is we did
not want each other until too late. Problem is I can't be
late for work in the morning. Problem is this morning
she says she dreamt she was holding a sandwich bag
of crickets. Problem is I am already late and listening
to the weather. Problem is we don't speak
to the problem. Problem is the school bus
that stops in front of our townhouse just as I'm reversing

the problem is we don't know who

Like, a girl on our lawn says, you want to hear me talk
like my sister when she's on the phone? Like she always
says *like*. Like this. Like me and my boyfriend
went to the mall and like I saw him looking at a girl
and like she was totawy into him. Like I can tell.
Like she was all, you know, like fwirting with him
like I wasn't there but like then I looked at her and she
like gave me a look like I can look at him if I want
to look at him, like they're my eyes. Like I got so mad
I like wanted to totawy kiw her.
                                        Like, my wife tells me
from her pillow in the dark, I am a pop can
with the tab broken and rattling around inside.
Like I might as well be a man. Like what is the point of

being a woman if you can't make another

So, a boy on our lawn says, I digged a hole
and put some water in it so my Transformer
could grow into a giant Transformer airplane gun
so when I shoot my laser *piu piu* I can fly away
up to the sun so you'll never catch me, so you'll never
shoot me, so you'll never ever ever ever ever ever
get me.
                                        So, my wife tells me
from her pillow in the dark, some of the crickets
in the sandwich bag were brittle — crickets are known
to eat their dead, you know — so I couldn't
be sure if I was eating dead or live crickets so I just
ate whatever my hand found so I must have eaten
some live ones so inside me sounded like night so as

baby you can see we will never have a

Then our child gets croup and turns us into raccoons.
Then our child gets better. Then our child starts chanting
in Latin and sneezing in Greek. Then our child walks
en pointe. Then our child has a crisis because it wants
to be a Komodo dragon in the school play but
only gets to be a lizard. Then our child falls asleep
in a chocolate factory. Then our child wakes up
in its teens. Then our child gets braces and glasses
and begins to glitter. Then our child smokes in the mirror.
Then our child leaves us. Then our child leaves us alone.
Then our child calls on Sunday. Then our child
meets someone else's child and has its own child.
Then our child brushes the nurses from our beds. Then

what happens to us what happens to our child is what happens to our child is

Please Print Clearly in Block Letters

Name. Permanent address. Mailing address (if different).
Will you want me when I ask you to vacuum the stairs
with the hose attachment? Daytime telephone number.
when we are eating cabbage for the third straight night?
Evening. Cell. Email. when you hear my footsteps
descend the basement stairs during the Leafs game?

Date of birth. Sex. Marital status. Will you want me
when birds walk across my face? Employment
in the last two years. and I give up mowing
my legs? From. To. give up dusting my cheeks?
From. To. give up Restylane?

                         Emergency
contact information. when I sit on the toilet seat
of the ensuite weeping? Name. over a clot of blood?
Relationship. over nothing? Telephone. Would you if I migrate
my mind into a key of winter afternoons from the Depression?
Type of card. Name on card. Card number. if I start calling
you Mr. Shopkeeper? Date of expiry. if I keep asking you if
you'll be getting any milk soon for the baby?

(Optional) Choose a security question. Would you want me
if I lose a limb? Mother's maiden name. if I lose a breast?
Year of father's birth. Will you want me when
I declare the above statements are true. I lose half of me?
Signature. Date. and half of you?

Missed Connections: Walmart Automotive Dept — w4m — (Lunenburg MA)

You. At the Tire and Lube Express. You said *lube*
and I — did you notice? — revved. Your name tag
was missing so I read your hair, curled like a string of e's,
your forearms drizzled with soft hairs like a boy's
first moustache. Apart from that, you were built
like a walrus. The kind of man that drives a Ford
pickup. Black or silver. You said, *There might be a gas leak*
and *We can't fix that here, but don't worry, we'll get you fixed.*
By *fixed* you meant *hooked up*, by *hooked up* you meant
in touch with and meant nothing beyond *touch*.

Me. Volvo. Smelled like gasoline: I overfilled the tank
before the oil change. I took the package that comes
with a filter replacement. Have you already forgotten me?
I had trouble with the debit machine. Remember? You said,
Turn your card the other way — remember? — and took my hand,
not the card, took my hand with the card in it
and swiped it through. Remember. Please.
The gasoline. The woman almost on fire.

Idioglossia

                                              Were we twins earlier
we might have saved the other from learning to speak,

to speak dead, to speak dead romance, to speak dead romance
languages. Utter embouchure. The aftertaste of hurt knots the
    tongue,

an unripe persimmon. An echo tumbles from the mountain range
of a French horn, hunt long finished, rabbits interrupted

by bullets. Then skinned. Then opened wide. There is no translation
for rescue save breath. How we speak to and only to each other.

By the routine of lung. After years of half-formed, airtight Hebrew
the lonely heart's grammar relaxes, allows one vowel. U.

American History I

Right. The fish. Right. The fish shakes its sequins
like an angry neck. Right. Small pond, backwater fish.
Right. Backward unicellular parents. Right. Who died
violently. Right. Aneurysms. Right. The fish grew
legs and walked right on shore. Right. It died
the first few times. Right. Natural causes. Right.
The time it didn't die it looked like a woman
climbing stairs to take teaspoons of cough syrup
to her child. Right. All the other times it looked
like a man. Right. Right. Right. Right. Its gills grew
into thalidomide arms. Right. It rolled around
like it was breading itself. Right. And said,
Ma, thinly, *Ma*. Right. Don't feel sorry for it. Right.
If a tree falls. Right. None of this happened
overnight, you understand. Right. It took millions
of years to grow a nose. Right. Then the rest
of the ocean emerged on ships. Right. Wearing hats.
Right. Hats. Right.

Satie's Gnossienne No. 3

Be careful early. And watch out
for the light that warns, *Seul, pendant un instant.*
You are. Happily ever.

A moment later you will be
tres perdu and will need to *ouvrez la tête*, whatever
that means.

A stepmother will leave you
in the forest until your nails grow into clefs. What
trouble

in the left hand,
the handful of dirt, the snowball of dirt, Satie
leaves for you.

He's having you,
necktied and heeled: you've been asked to go
to a museum,

an exhibit of female torsos
made from breadcrumbs, that sort of thing.
People go *mm* in their throats.

If you take Satie seriously,
then you hear grief, just the far corner of it,
and separate from you:

the snoring — or is it moaning —
woman in the hospital bed next to the friend
you came to see.

Personal History I, Canon

Many options, many options. Copy. Multifunctional,
you could say. Copy. You could say, I've been fun. Copy.
Off and on. Copy. I can staple a bow in my hair. Copy. I'd prefer
not to. Copy. But I'm not particular. Copy. I read everything
you give me. Copy. Closely. Copy. I know, for instance,
that the footer of the email from the immigration attorney
was appended by a Blackberry Wireless Device. Copy.
I read everything you give me. Copy. Money. Copy.
What I don't like I eat or spit up. Copy. I am not acting
like a child. You're a child. Copy. Once the toner
cartridge exploded in the room behind the secretaries.
Copy. And a licensed technician came in and talked
to me for an hour. Copy. *How did that make you feel?*
and so on. Copy. I will jam occasionally, arbitrarily
bite your hand. Copy. Gemini. Copy. Two-sided. Copy.
Old man with wrinkled dugs. Copy. Who knows what.
Copy. I read everything. Copy. I read everything. Copy.
Copy. Copy.

Personal History II, Fugue

— there was cause for alarm — I can help — at thirty —
the next person — thirty-five — in line — and forty —
over here — I ran out of my body — I can help —
and watched fire trucks — the next person — scream and spit —
in line — over my faulty wiring — over this way —
and when finally boarded up — I can help — condemned —
the next person — spray-painted in the night by teenagers
in sagging jeans — standing in line — I thought maybe
that we could actually like totally you know — this way —
basically — I can help — there was nothing I could say —
the next person — there was nothing — in line — I could say —
over here — there was cause for alarm — I can help — the building
dreams of the marks of children ascending up the doorframe
year after year — the next person in line — Dylan age three
and four and five — over here — but — no one and ever — I can
    help —
copy — the next person — no one and ever — I can help —
what? — over here — I can — no one and ever — help — right —
I can — no one and ever — help

ABOUT THE POETS

FADY JOUDAH is a practising physician of internal medicine and an award-winning poet and translator. Among his translations are two poetry collections by Mahmoud Darwish, *The Butterfly's Burden* and *If I Were Another*, for which he won the 2010 PEN USA Literary Award. He lives in Houston, Texas.

JENNIFER MAIDEN has published sixteen collections of poetry; her book *Pirate Rain* won the Age Poetry Book of the Year Award and the NSW Premier's Kenneth Slessor Prize for Poetry. She is a recipient of the Christopher Brennan Award for lifetime achievement.

DAVID W. MCFADDEN began writing poetry in 1956 and began publishing poetry in 1958. *Why Are You So Sad? Selected Poems of David W. McFadden* was shortlisted for the 2008 Griffin Poetry Prize, and *Be Calm, Honey* was shortlisted for the 2009 Governor General's Literary Award for Poetry. McFadden is the author of about thirty-five books of poetry, fiction, and travel writing. He lives in Toronto, Ontario.

JAMES POLLOCK's poems have been published in *AGNI*, *The Paris Review*, *Poetry Daily*, and more than a dozen other journals. His critical reviews have appeared in *Contemporary Poetry Review*, *Books in Canada*, *The New Quarterly*, and in a collection of his criticism, *You Are Here: Essays on the Art of Poetry in Canada*. He is an associate professor at Loras College in Dubuque, Iowa, where he teaches poetry in the creative writing program. He lives in Madison, Wisconsin.

ALAN SHAPIRO's recent collection *Old War* won the 2009 Ambassador Book Award. A National Book Critics Circle Award finalist and winner of the *Los Angeles Times* Book Prize, Shapiro is the William R. Kenan Jr. Distinguished Professor of English and Creative Writing at the University of North Carolina, Chapel Hill.

BRENDA SHAUGHNESSY was born in Okinawa, Japan, and grew up in southern California. She is the author of *Human Dark with Sugar*, winner of the James Laughlin Award and a finalist for the National Book Critics Circle Award, and *Interior with Sudden Joy*. Shaughnessy's poems have appeared in *Best American Poetry*, *Harper's*, *The Nation*, *The New Yorker*, *The Paris Review*, and *The Rumpus*. She is an assistant professor of English at Rutgers University, Newark, and lives in Brooklyn, New York, with her husband, son, and daughter.

IAN WILLIAMS' previous books are *Not Anyone's Anything* and *You Know Who You Are*. He is the winner of the 2011 Danuta Gleed Literary Award for the best first English-language collection of short fiction, a finalist for the ReLit Prize for poetry, and was named as one of ten Canadian writers to watch by CBC. His writing has appeared in *The Fiddlehead, Arc, Contemporary Verse 2, Rattle, jubilat, Confrontation, The Antigonish Review, Gargoyle, Folio, Pebble Lake Review, Callaloo, Descant*, and *Matrix Magazine*. Williams completed his Ph.D. in English at the University of Toronto and works as an English professor. He currently lives in Brampton, Ontario.

Palestinian poet GHASSAN ZAQTAN is a novelist, editor, and the author of ten collections of poetry. He was born in Beit Jala, near Bethlehem, and has lived in Jordan, Beirut, Damascus, and Tunis. He returned to Palestine in 1994 and now lives in Ramallah.

ACKNOWLEDGEMENTS

The publisher thanks the following for their kind permission to reprint the work contained in this volume:

"Hillary and Eleanor 9: The Pearl Roundabout," "In the International Pavilion," "Diary Poem: Uses of Liquid Nitrogen," and "My heart has an Embassy" from *Liquid Nitrogen* by Jennifer Maiden are reprinted by permission of Giramondo Publishing.

"Stimulation Galore," "Funny Country," "Workout at the Why," and "Microscopic Surgery" from *What's the Score?* by David W. McFadden are reprinted by permission of Mansfield Press.

"Northwest Passage," "The Poet at Seven," "Ex Patria," "House," "The Museum of Death," "Northwest Passage," and "Map of the Interior" from *Sailing to Babylon* by James Pollock are reprinted by permission of Able Muse Press.

"Gas Station Restroom," "Car Dealership at 3 A.M.," "Hotel Lobby," "Stone Church," "Funeral Home," "Beloved," and "Faucet" from *Night of the Republic* by Alan Shapiro are reprinted by permission of Houghton Mifflin Harcourt.

"Artless," "All Possible Pain," "Liquid Flesh," "Hearth" from *Our Andromeda* by Brenda Shaughnessy are reprinted by permission of Copper Canyon Press.

"Rings," "Please Print Clearly in Block Letters," "Missed Connections: Walmart Automotive Dept — w4m — (Lunenberg MA)," "Idioglossia," "American History I," "Satie's Gnossienne No. 3," "Personal History I, Canon," and "Personal History II, Fugue" from *Personals* by Ian Williams are reprinted by permission of Freehand Books.

"The Dead in the Garden," "Black Horses," "An Enemy Comes Down the Hill," "The Orchard's Song," "The Bird Follows Me," and "Everything As It Was" from *Like a Straw Bird It Follows Me, and Other Poems* by Ghassan Zaqtan, translated by Fady Joudah, are reprinted by permission of Yale University Press.

THE 2013 GRIFFIN POETRY PRIZE ANTHOLOGY

The best books of poetry published in English internationally and in Canada are honoured each year with the $65,000 Griffin Poetry Prize, one of the world's most prestigious and valuable literary awards. Since 2001 this annual prize has acted as a tremendous spur to interest in and recognition of poetry, focusing worldwide attention on the formidable talent of poets writing in English. Each year the editor of *The Griffin Poetry Prize Anthology* gathers the work of the extraordinary poets shortlisted for the awards and introduces us to some of the finest poems in their collections.

This year, editor and prize juror Suzanne Buffam's selections from the international shortlist include poems from Jennifer Maiden's *Liquid Nitrogen* (Giramondo Publishing), Alan Shapiro's *Night of the Republic* (Houghton Mifflin Harcourt), Brenda Shaughnessy's *Our Andromeda* (Copper Canyon Press), and Ghassan Zaqtan's *Like a Straw Bird It Follows Me, and Other Poems* (Yale University Press), translated by Fady Joudah. The selections from the Canadian shortlist include poems from David W. McFadden's *What's the Score?* (Mansfield Press), *Sailing to Babylon* by James Pollock (Able Muse Press), and *Personals* by Ian Williams (Freehand Books).

In choosing the 2013 shortlist, prize jurors Suzanne Buffam, Mark Doty, and Wang Ping considered more than 500 collections published in the previous year. The jury also wrote the citations that introduce the seven poets' nominated works.

Royalties generated from *The 2013 Griffin Poetry Prize Anthology* will be donated to UNESCO's World Poetry Day, which was created to support linguistic diversity through poetic expression and to offer endangered languages the opportunity to be heard in their communities.

The Griffin Trust

Margaret Atwood
Carolyn Forché
Scott Griffin
Robert Hass
Michael Ondaatje
Robin Robertson
David Young